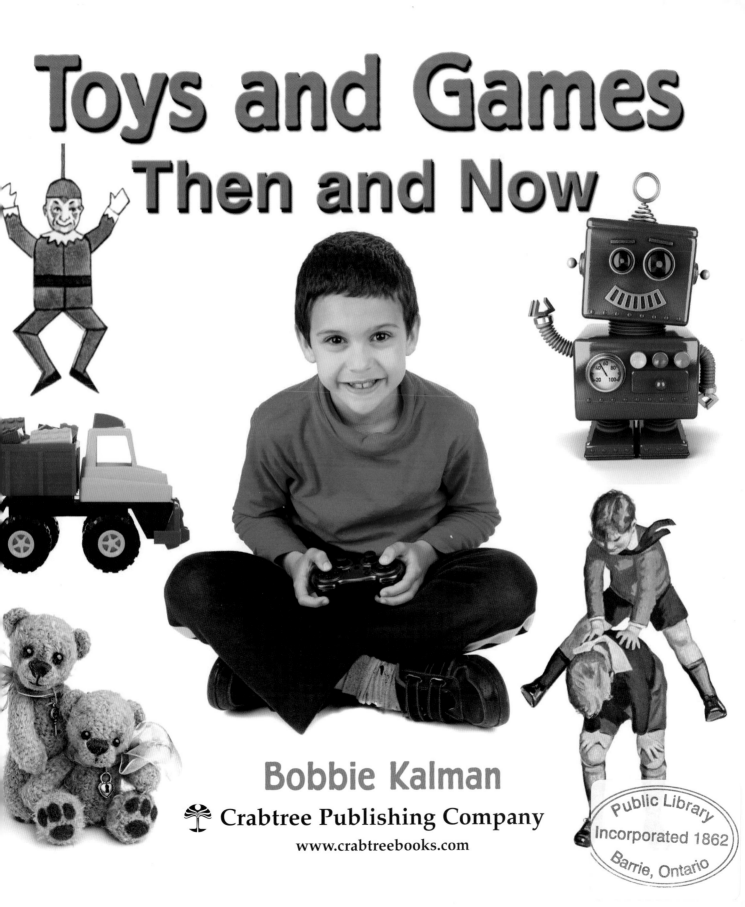

Toys and Games
Then and Now

Bobbie Kalman

🍄 Crabtree Publishing Company

www.crabtreebooks.com

Created by Bobbie Kalman

Dedicated by Katherine Berti
To Damian Lee Berti,
our little bundle of joy and radiant sunshine.
Mommy and Daddy love you with all our hearts.

Author and Editor-in-Chief
Bobbie Kalman

Editors
Kathy Middleton
Crystal Sikkens

Photo research
Bobbie Kalman

Design
Bobbie Kalman
Samantha Crabtree
Katherine Berti
Samara Parent (front cover)

Prepress technician
Katherine Berti

Print coordinator
Margaret Amy Salter

Illustrations and reproductions
Barbara Bedell: front and back cover, pages 5, 7 (top right), 10
(middle right), 13 (bottom left), 15, 16, 17, 19, 21 (right), 22
Circa Art: pages 1 (top left and bottom right), 7 (bottom right)
Allan and Deborah Drew-Brook-Cormack: page 21 (left)
Bonna Rouse: page 13 (bottom right)
Wikimedia Commons: page 10 (top left)

Photographs
Thinkstock: pages 6 (middle right, border), 10 (bottom right),
11 (middle and bottom), 12 (bottom left), 13 (top right),
14 (background), 16 (bottom right), 17 (bottom right),
19 (border), 22 (all)
Other images by Shutterstock, including photographs on cover

Library and Archives Canada Cataloguing in Publication

Kalman, Bobbie, author
    Toys and games then and now / Bobbie Kalman.

(From olden days to modern ways in your community)
Includes index.
Issued in print and electronic formats.
ISBN 978-0-7787-0128-6 (bound).--ISBN 978-0-7787-0210-8 (pbk.).
--ISBN 978-1-4271-9417-6 (pdf).--ISBN 978-1-4271-9411-4 (html)

        1. Toys--Juvenile literature. 2. Games--Juvenile literature.
I. Title.

GV1203.K35 2013   j790.1'922   C2013-906094-4
                                             C2013-906095-2

Library of Congress Cataloging-in-Publication Data

Kalman, Bobbie.
    Toys and games then and now / Bobbie Kalman.
        pages cm. -- (From olden days to modern ways in your community)
    Includes index.
    ISBN 978-0-7787-0128-6 (reinforced library binding) -- ISBN 978-0-7787-0210-8 (pbk.)
-- ISBN 978-1-4271-9417-6 (electronic pdf) -- ISBN 978-1-4271-9411-4 (electronic html)
    1. Toys--History--Juvenile literature. 2. Games--History--Juvenile literature.
I. Title.

GV1218.5.K34 2013
790.1'33--dc23

                                             2013034934

Crabtree Publishing Company
www.crabtreebooks.com   1-800-387-7650

Printed in Canada/012014/BF20131120

Published in Canada
Crabtree Publishing
616 Welland Ave.
St. Catharines, Ontario
L2M 5V6

Published in the United States
Crabtree Publishing
PMB 59051
350 Fifth Avenue, 59th Floor
New York, New York 10118

Published in the United Kingdom
Crabtree Publishing
Maritime House
Basin Road North, Hove
BN41 1WR

Published in Australia
Crabtree Publishing
3 Charles Street
Coburg North
VIC 3058

What is in this book?

Long ago and today

Children today have a choice of many toys and games. They play with toys and games for fun, but they also learn skills, such as reading and writing, while they play. Children play at home, at school, and outdoors.

Spinning hoops is great exercise!

Video games help children pay attention.

This puzzle mat helps children learn to spell.

How did they play?

Long ago, there were few toys and no video games. Children also had less time to play because they had to help their parents work on the farm or around the house. Children still had fun playing, however. At work parties called **bees**, they played with the other children after they helped their parents work.

This ring-tossing game was called Graces. It helped children develop balance.

Farmers cut down hay to feed to their animals. Large bundles of hay created paths where children could run and play hiding games at a work party.

Popular toys

Today, children have a lot of time to play. Each year, new kinds of toys are made for them to enjoy. Many of the new toys are similar to the kinds of toys their parents and grandparents played with long ago.

Ask your parents what toys they played with when they were kids. Which of their toys were the same or similar to yours?

Toys from the past

Popular toys in the past were dolls, dollhouses, building blocks, and a toy called Noah's Ark. The toy was based on a Bible story in which Noah built an **ark**, or giant boat, because a great flood was coming. Noah took two of every kind of animal on the boat. The Noah's Ark toy had several animals.

Many people went to church on Sunday. On this day, children were allowed to play with only a few toys, such as the Noah's Ark toy.

dollhouse

doll and carriage

Girls played with dolls, but boys played with toy soldiers like these.

7

Toys with power

Many toys today are powered by batteries or electricity. Some have **remote controls**. Children use remote controls to make helicopters fly, give robots directions, or play video games. Which of your toys have remote controls?

The helicopter above and the robot on the left are both operated by remote controls.

remote control

How did these toys move?

Long ago, there was no electricity, batteries, or remote controls. Some toys, like the robot and duck below, were wound like clocks. That is why they were called **clockwork toys**. Small wheels inside the toys helped them move for a short time.

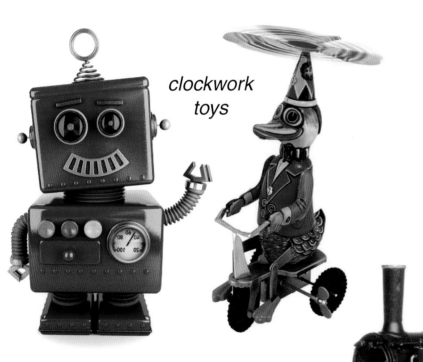

clockwork toys

The jack-in-the-box toy was a box with a crank. As children turned the crank, a melody played—usually "Pop Goes the Weasel." As the song played, a clown popped up at different times, surprising the children.

Some old toy trains had wind-up controls, and others had real steam engines.

Old games still played

This girl from long ago and the boy below from today are playing dominoes in different ways.

There are many kinds of word and number games that have been played by children for hundreds of years. Dominoes, Anagrams, and other word games are still fun to play.

This boy uses the domino tiles to learn numbers.

In the game of Anagrams, children move letters around to make new words.

Board games

Games such as Snakes and Ladders, checkers, and chess are very old board games. Which ones do you like to play?

Checkers teaches these girls to think and make decisions. It is also a lot of fun.

Snakes and Ladders is a very old game that came from India. Do you play this fun board game?

chessboard

Chess is played by two players. Each player has 16 pieces. The king is the most important. Players try to capture each other's pieces, especially the king.

Classroom games

Long ago, the main subjects taught in school were language arts and math. These are also the main subjects taught today. There are many games that help teach these subjects to children. Some of these games can be played on **digital tablets**.

This teacher makes spelling fun to learn.

This boy enjoys reading books and playing math games on his tablet.

Fun to learn

Long ago, children who lived in the country went to one-room schools. Children of all ages were taught in the same classroom by one teacher. There were not many school supplies, so the teacher used games to make learning fun.

*An **abacus** helped young children add and subtract.*

This math game was called Buzz. When the teacher said the word "buzz," the children had to say the correct number. Which numbers have been replaced by buzzing bees? What do the numbers have in common?

This girl is writing a science story. What will she write about these plants and animals?

13

Outdoor fun

The children on these pages are having fun in similar ways. The kids on this page are enjoying the games played by children long ago.

These girls are playing leapfrog. How do you play it?

This game of tug-of-war is being played at the beach. Where do you play it?

What game do you think this girl is playing?

How did they play?

Leapfrog and Sardines were two popular games. To play Sardines, one person hides, while the rest, called seekers, count. When a seeker finds the hider, they both hide in the same place. Eventually, everyone except the last seeker is in the same hiding place. Will the last seeker find the hiders on the right?

To play leapfrog, the players line up behind one another and leap over the person in front.

Why is this game called Sardines?

The goal of tug-of-war is to pull the opposing team over a line on the ground.

Sports then and now

lacrosse

Many of the sports that are played today are like the sports played long ago. Baseball became a favorite sport in the 1850s. Football is a combination of rugby and soccer. In the 1870s, players started carrying footballs instead of just kicking them. Other sports played then and now are badminton, hockey, and lacrosse. Lacrosse was learned from the Native people. It is still a very popular sport, especially in Canada.

Tackling is a big part of rugby as well as football.

Football players today carry the ball and run with it.

shuttlecock

battledore

The girl on the left is playing Battledore and Shuttlecock, a game that is known as badminton today. The girl on the right is playing badminton.

shuttle or birdie

racket

The boys above are playing Shinny, also known as "street hockey." It was played in fields, as well as on ice.

hockey

Rolling on wheels

Rolling on wheels is great exercise! Scooters, skateboards, in-line skates, and bicycles all roll on wheels. Many children enjoy the thrill of mountain biking, which takes them over rough areas without roads, such as hills. What safety equipment should you wear when you do these sports? Which child is not riding safely?

skateboard

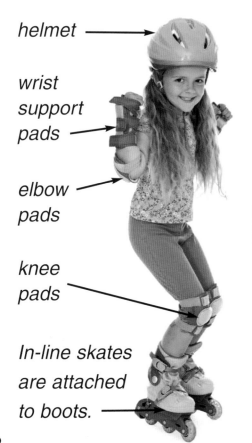

helmet

wrist support pads

elbow pads

knee pads

In-line skates are attached to boots.

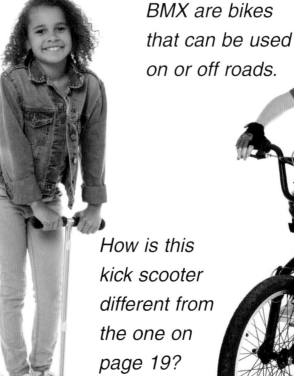

How is this kick scooter different from the one on page 19?

BMX are bikes that can be used on or off roads.

Bikes, scooters, and roller skates

Many early bicycles had a huge front wheel. This kind of bike was called a **velocipede**, which means "fast foot" in French. Very few children had bicycles because they were expensive. Instead, children rode scooters, which had a long handle with handlebars, and a footboard with a wheel at each end. They also used roller skates, which they strapped onto their shoes. There were no skateboards until the 1950s.

velocipede

roller skates

To ride her scooter, this girl kicks the ground and then jumps on.

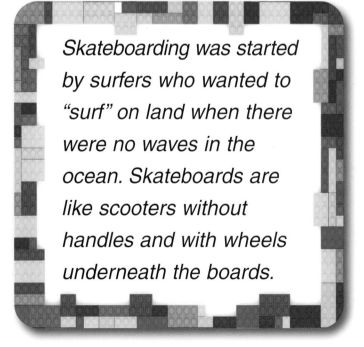

Skateboarding was started by surfers who wanted to "surf" on land when there were no waves in the ocean. Skateboards are like scooters without handles and with wheels underneath the boards.

19

Party games

People throw parties because they want to have fun with their family and friends. They hold parties to celebrate birthdays, weddings, Halloween, Thanksgiving, New Year's Eve, and religious holidays like Christmas and Hanukkah. What games do you play at parties? Which are your favorite games?

Breaking a piñata is a popular birthday and Christmas game that came from Mexico but is now practiced in many countries. A piñata is a decorated container filled with small toys or candy, or both. It is hung from a rope, and children who are blindfolded take turns hitting it with a stick until it breaks. When the treats fall on the ground, the children rush to collect them.

Bobbing for apples is often played at Halloween parties (see next page).

Parties long ago

People long ago had fewer ways to entertain themselves, so they often got together with family and friends. At **harvest** parties during autumn, children played many kinds of apple games. Bobbing for apples was a fun game—both for the "bobbers" and the people watching them. Apples float and bounce around in water, so biting into them without holding them is difficult.

bag filled with treats

child with blindfold

Bag and Stick was popular at Christmas parties. It was broken the same way that a piñata is broken.

Parlor games

Many large homes had **parlors**. A parlor was the best room in a house. Guests were invited into this room, and games called **parlor games** were played there. The Cobweb Game was a children's parlor game played by many families during the Christmas holidays. To play this game, colorful ribbons were attached to a metal spider that hung from the ceiling. The ribbons were part of the game and also decorated the room.

The ribbons were wound around the room in a tangled web. They were pulled under, over, and behind the furniture. Each child followed one colored ribbon from the spider to its end, where his or her present was hidden.

Learn more

Books

(Sports starters series). Crabtree Publishing, 2007–2013.

Kalman, Bobbie and Heather Levigne. *Schoolyard Games* (Historic Communities) Crabtree Publishing, 2001.

Kalman, Bobbie and Heather Levigne. *Classroom Games* (Historic Communities) Crabtree Publishing, 2001.

(Sports in Action series). Crabtree Publishing, 2000–2012.

Kalman, Bobbie. *Games from Long Ago* (Historic Communities) Crabtree Publishing, 1995.

Kalman, Bobbie and David Schimpky. *Old-Time Toys* (Historic Communities) Crabtree Publishing, 1995.

Websites

Learn more about the different games in the olden days at:
http://mrsgebauer.com/oldfalls/games/games.htm

Find out more about toys and games played long ago and today:
www.sagessite.com/games_long_ago_and_today.htm

Words to know

Note: Some boldfaced words are defined where they appear in the book.

abacus A math tool with a wire frame containing beads that slide

ark A large boat from the Bible built by Noah to save himself, his family, and two of every kind of animal from a flood

bee A gathering of people that worked on a project together

clockwork toy A toy that is wound like a clock in order to run or do certain motions for a short time

digital tablet A portable computer that operates by touching the screen

harvest The time during which crops were cut down and gathered

parlor A room in which people received and entertained guests

parlor games Games played in the parlor of someone's home

remote control A device used to control a machine from a certain distance away

velocipede An old bicycle with a large front wheel

Index